SHOWTIME AT THE MINISTRY OF LOST CAUSES

PITT POETRY SERIES | Ed Ochester, *Editor*

SHOW TIME at the MINISTRY of LOST CAUSES

Cheryl Dumesnil

UNIVERSITY OF PITTSBURGH PRESS

Published by the University of Pittsburgh Press, Pittsburgh, Pa., 15260

Copyright © 2016, Cheryl Dumesnil

All rights reserved

Manufactured in the United States of America

Printed on acid-free paper

10 9 8 7 6 5 4 3 2 1

ISBN 13: 978-0-8229-6431-5

ISBN 10: 0-8229-6431-7

Cover art and design by Joel W. Coggins

For Marilyn and Robert Dumesnil,
with relentless gratitude

Do you have the patience to wait
till your mud settles and the water is clear?
Lao-Tzu

—

All that noise coming in.
You have to make use of it somehow.
Grace Paley

CONTENTS

IV. THAT I COULD KEEP YOU LIKE THIS

V. THE ACROBATS OF PITTSBURGH

SHOWTIME AT THE MINISTRY OF LOST CAUSES

I. GOOD MORNING HEARTACHE

It's not the Holy Spirit

letting up out of an oil-slicked puddle
between the tracks on 9th Ave,

that feathered blur flashing
toward the N-Judah's windshield.

It's only a rock dove, tail fan
splayed, pewter wings spread

wide, reversing direction mid-air.
But tell me, what better prayer

than this? The near miss, the heart
shocked awake, that bird rising

over sooted buildings, gated doors.

The Flock

That there are too many birds—I know this already.
But the buckshot-pierced dove's open mouth

echoed my lover's sleep-slackened jaw, so I
covered its body with leaves and swore off

my rifle forever. And if I decided love was possible
because her eyelashes iridesced like peacock feathers,

so be it. If a house sparrow arrives on my sill,
sprig of language pinched in her beak, who am I

to tell her no? The first time I saw the plastic owl
perched on my San Francisco rooftop, I circled

the building three times, awed by the fog-hazed
visitation. The window-stunned robin who hunkered

on my deck for hours—that she flew away meant
one thing, that she left a red stain meant another.

Revolution

Nahr al-Bared, 2007

After a night of mortar fire,
in the first light, her father drags

a hose across his yard, to water
the plum saplings he planted

last month. Half a world away,
crepe myrtles outside her home

blaze, impotent red blooms.
When she phones, he will talk

only about the plums, how
sweet they will taste, sliced

and salted, on his favorite plate.

The Red-Shouldered Hawk, the Raven

A turkey vulture turns one last revolution
around its cobalt plain, while we hike

a ridge trail complicated by oak galls,
exposed roots. Tonight we have traded

radio station polemics for this: the white
crescent rising over the canyon lip is not

an interrogator's bulb, but an urn spilling
truths the red-shouldered hawk, the raven

have always known. How many words
does it take to roll a boulder from a cave's

mouth? How much ink to write history
on that water? Out here the night wind

strips us of all illusion, identification cards
ripped up and scattered for Gretel's birds.

When there's no money left—

none for killing the termites
lunching on the barn siding, none

for painting the weather-eaten
porch, or righting the rain gutter

that sags like a half-paralyzed
mouth, say it again: *We are lucky*

to have a house. Under *Job Skills*,
list: *balloon animals, roller disco,*

alchemy of opposing truths.
Under *Personal References*, write:

After the night of a thousand
lightning strikes, ask the first

bird who calls out for dawn.

Good Morning Heartache

That bastard sun rises again, dissolving
the only good dream I've had all year.

My waking mind feels for hope, blind
reach for eyeglasses on the nightstand

or an oxygen regulator fallen
from my mouth to the ocean floor.

Across town, my friend can't lift her head
off her pillow, the chemo eating her

platelets and maybe the tumor, while
in my kitchen, the coffee timer clicks on,

French Roast draining into the carafe.
On the news, a Somali mother searches

tree bark for emaciated insects: *You see,*
even the bugs are starving. Dear world,

what good can you offer? The finches'
red-breasted tune, these strawberries

grown fat around dimpled gold seeds?
My son, she brushes dust from his lips,

he keeps asking for a donut. Just a nibble
of a donut. I don't know what to say.

Showtime at the Ministry of Lost Causes

On the corner of North Main and Bonanza,
Sandy busks for change, her rope-yellow hair

gone weeks without water, sun-chapped lips
mouthing a rusted harmonica. Give her

a cup of coffee, she'll call you *broken
blue wing*. Ask her where she comes from,

she'll sing, her voice a forest full of birds
you can't name:

*You got field mice in your corn palace,
    ain't nothin' you can do.*

*Field mice in the corn palace,
    ain't nothin' you can do.*

*Melancholy's comin' for you,
    better put down your broom.*

*Y'all die a little every day,
    go 'head now, put down your broom.*

Colossal Failure of Human Design, We Celebrate the 100th Anniversary of Your Death

What no god could sink
sunk, and so we trace

our fingers along the filigree
of your demise, imagine

Wallace Hartley's eight
musicians dragging notes

out of their instruments,
like soldiers begging

their dying comrades
to breathe. *And the band*

played on, not because
of some contract loyalty

or ethic of bravery,
but because they knew

the only way to enter
death is as the cello's

body reverberating
the bow's final stroke.

Ode to October

Who needs a cathedral, October, when you
bring us this light? In the grocery store parking lot,

rush hour shoppers stream toward the doors,
their silhouettes edged in gold, whole body halos

radiating as they tug carts from the line, search
pockets for lists. Who needs a confessional,

October, when you are here, illuminating all
my sins? Yes, sometimes I love my wife poorly.

Yes, sometimes I forget my children are sacred.
Yes, my capacity for beauty will fail me, fail

you, always—I have no saxophone to accompany
your impossible timbres, no Raw Sienna or

Cerulean Blue shining wet on canvas. And yes,
I know the story: a young monk spent a night

in a cave, fanged cobra blocking his exit. Hours
in terror he shook, until dawn lit the archway,

erasing the snake. I suspect that was your work, too,
October. You dotting morning's grass blades

with silver beads. You calling my heart a black walnut
hidden under autumn's leaves. You daring me

to believe, if I pried the locked seam open,
I'd find your light there too, rendering even that

rotting meat gossamer-laced, necessary.

II. AT THE REUNION OF LOST MEMORIES

—

Tampons: A Memoir

I. *Mystery*

Belly flopping on Mom's bed while she unpacked
her American Tourister, I slid my hand inside
the silky interior pocket and pulled out
a paper-sheathed Tampax. *What's this?* I asked,
pressing my nostrils to one end and sniffing
the length of it, like an aficionado
testing his cigar. Some new candy?
A sachet? She snatched it from my hand:
You don't need to know about that yet,
and stashed that mystery in her bathroom drawer.

II. *Aisle 6 Feminine Hygiene Products*

Why not demystify the tampon?
Identify it for what it is: the most
underused craft supply in Martha
Stewart's repertoire. Pull that albino
mouse out of its tube and hot glue
pink ears, dot eyes with a Sharpie,
pin whiskers on the nose. Apply
a generous coat of gray acrylic and
those leftover cylinders make perfect
smoke stacks for the fifth-grader's
diorama of the Industrial Revolution.
For summer fun, slap the bottom
of that rocket launcher, watch it
soar over the back fence, unfurling
its white flag in the sky.

III. *Shock*

Toxic Shock Syndrome sounded like something
that happened to girls who swam in dirty water
during a lightning storm. *You can get it from touching
a door knob,* the news anchor warned. The brass handle
on the living room door gleamed, suspect. *Are tampons
killing women?* the headline asked. My mother said,
I'm glad you're too young to have to worry about this.

IV. *Seventh Grade*

Ripping the crepe-thin paper open,
I stared at the wide cotton tip
then looked down at my wispy-haired self.
That can't possibly fit in me.

V. *College*

In my dream a steeping teabag
turned into a used tampon
just before I took a sip, blood
staining the water pink. I woke
and spent two hours trying
to use the image in a poem:
a ribbon slowly unweaving itself,
crimson cloud storming the mug.

VI. *Miscarriage*

When we found out the embryo was dead
but hadn't left my body, the doctor

named our wanted baby *missed abortion*.
An unfortunate medical term, the nurse

confirmed. Back home, I loaded four pills
on a tampon's retracted tip, slid them in.

My wife stroked my hair as we lay in bed,
waiting for the medicine to send

that corpse floating out on a river of red.

VII. *Progesterone Supplements*

The endocrinologist called to tell me
to push the capsules I used to take orally
into my vagina instead. I balked: *Really?*
These? He delivered a mini lecture
on the absorption power of vaginal
tissue, and I remembered the toxic shock
scare of my childhood, stories about
asbestos in tampons, the reason I use
the organic, unbleached cotton brand.
To punctuate his point, the doc asked,
Wanna know what crack addicts do?
I didn't. I pushed the magic drug
between my southern lips and hoped
it was enough to keep the next baby alive.

VIII. *Monday Morning*

The two-year-old finds a box of tampons
under the bathroom sink, tears one open.

His mama and I look at each other and shrug.
We continue blow-drying hair,

applying mascara. Meanwhile, little guy
dismantles his toy and offers half to big brother,

who sticks the tube between his lips: *Look,*
it's a smoke. He parades around our bedroom,

flicking ashes, while baby brother lifts a white
cardboard microphone to his mouth and sings,

Get up, stand up. Stand up for your rights,
wiggling naked hips in the mirrored closet doors.

Conception Myth

First of all, there's no turkey baster,
just this needleless syringe and a plastic vial

with a salmon-colored frozen pellet
at the bottom, no bigger than the tip

of my pinky finger. The label promises
twenty-four-thousand swimmers

will emerge when the ice defrosts. We need
only one. And it seems easy, like that

carnival game where you shoot water
into the clown's open mouth and a balloon

blooms out of its head. Until we see
that movie where sperm weave like drunken

mole rats, bumping into fallopian walls
while the egg sits on her barstool, sipping

a last-call vodka, checking her watch.
Post-insemination, the bowl of my pelvis

warms like a room full of bodies, and I
wonder if one, which one will wander

down that hallway, hear her whispering
behind the closed door, and knock.

On Air Guitar, Lip Gloss, and Flat Irons

The guy playing air guitar in the back seat of this bus—
Raiders beanie pulled down over iPod ear buds, invisible

pick pinched between right thumb and pointer, left hand
trembling along the ghost frets—I didn't realize

people still do that in their thirties. But there he is,
auburn goatee etched with gray, reminding me

of my first middle school dance where Tina Colbert
and I jammed with Eddie Van Halen, our hair

whipping like willows in a rainstorm, arms windmilling
over our make-believe Stratocasters. Sure, it seems

awkward now, but at the time it beat the alternatives:
whispering behind cupped hands, or comparing lip gloss

brands with the girls in the restroom line where
Keri Orton rubbed her Dr. Pepper–flavored Bonne Bell

under her nose, then wore a glistening mustache
all night because she liked the scent. Sixth graders,

we were on the verge of being self-conscious about
such things, and I felt sorry for her, for not knowing

how stupid that looked. A few months later I learned
an average make-up wearing woman will ingest

the equivalent of three tubes of lipstick a year, simply
by licking her lips, which is why I'm still conflicted

about cosmetics. And flat irons. Standing in front
of a mirror for forty-five minutes each morning, I wonder,

*What else could I do with all this time? With all
the collective time burned up by all the flat irons*

in all the bathrooms in the world, what could we do?
Sometimes while the oils smoke off my hair, I think up

poems, like this one. But not right now. No, right now
I am riding this bus around the downtown loop

because it makes my kids happy. There they are,
sitting up on their knees, gripping the seat back,

squealing over sightings of garbage trucks, water fountains
and parking lot gates—the trifecta for these suburban

boys who keep stealing glances at the air guitarist,
but he has switched to drums now, arms crossed

at the wrists, hands gripping pretend sticks. Secretly
I worry the kids will ask me what he's doing. What

would I say? Eyes closed, knit cap bobbing, he is the master
of this grand stage, a musician magician hammering

out of this moment so much more than what it is.

At the Reunion of Lost Memories

High School snorts Ritalin in a bathroom stall,
smears lipstick across the back of her hand,

snags her stiletto in her skirt hem, tears it
while slam dancing with the custodian's assistant.

Streamers droop from the ballroom ceiling,
crepe eels lolling in the fan breeze.

Fifth Grade hocks a loogie in the fruit punch
while College works hard to recall names,

anyone's names. Who painted Air Force insignias
on his '64 Mustang? Whose kiss felt like

a dead slug in her mouth? Which sorority
sister got caught poaching care packages

from the dormitory mail room? *Nothing
to worry about*, Old Age whispers, *this is just*

how it goes: even the good ones get lost—
the midwife who caught your first baby,

the coworker who let you sleep on her couch
after your divorce. At the podium, Midlife

taps the microphone, clears her throat—this was,
after all, her idea: the chicken croquettes,

the all-star band. She wants to explain why
she's called everyone here, but before she can speak,

Etta James saunters onstage, croons, *At last* . . .
In a botched confetti drop, ripped-up secrets

flutter down, accumulating on the polyester rug,
like the snow that fell and fell that one spring day,

cloaking all the cars, covering their tracks.

When she finally lost the weight

she couldn't wait to dress like a slut—
spandex micro-mini tank dress,

black lace stockings hiding
telltale stretch mark scars,

her hipbones protruding like tiny
fight-the-power fists.

>*You've lost weight,*
>*are you okay?*

>*I did this on purpose.*

>*Oh good, I thought you might be sick.*

Three months of two
hundred calories

a day. Oh heady
 ecstasy of living

on five apple slices
 and twenty-four

peanuts, four liters
 of Diet Cherry Coke.

Oh heady ecstasy
 of shrinkage and control.

Fantastic!
[Arm slithers around waist, tugs in.]
You're looking great!
[Whispers]
Will you tell my daughter
how you did it? She's grown
                    so fat.

Ode to Pink Floyd

You were the perfect soundtrack for our theater
of discontent—two honors students stoned

on Acapulco Gold, scribbling "We don't need no
thought control" in the margins our Western Civilization

text books, or sprawled on my dorm room floor, testing
the elasticity of words like *lost* and *soul* and *mate*

and *found*, "Dark Side of the Moon" reverberating
the windows. Pink Floyd, what would we have done

without "How I Wish You Were Here" recorded
on cassettes we exchanged when winter break sent us

back to our families? Rewind. Play. Rewind. Play.
Rewind. Play. Until those tapes thinned and snapped.

You were there, too, Pink Floyd, when we reunited,
hunched on the curb outside 7-11, spooning cola

Slurpees and strawberry Pop-Tarts into each other's
mouths, the apple I had carved into a pipe, still warm

in my pocket. Man, how we could talk for hours
about desperation and sunsets. And those parking lot

rats fighting over a greasy churros wrapper—
how they shape-shifted into a revelatory metaphor

for greed. See, Pink Floyd, it was just like you said:
we're all rodents, god damn it, fucking rats,

as if your lyrics transcribed the invisible scripts
of our minds, words trailing like jet streams across

that bruised-up January sky. For real. Sweet Pink
Floyd, forgive me, it's true: I lost all your CDs

in the break-up. Vinyl, too. Dust-caked and packed
in the Berkeley Farms milk crate we had carried

cross-country and back. Twenty years later, dear
Pink Floyd, the kids we were are filed in my memory

under the heading *Teenage Melodrama*, cross-reference
Pathetic Fallacy. But somehow even here, you find me,

Pink Floyd, "On the Turning Away" sent through my car
radio like the ghost voice of a beloved long dead,

so haunting I have to pull over to the shoulder
and listen: oh spectacular juxtaposition of pontification

and power cords, oh gospel choir of Cannabis-enlightened
youth, I am your prodigal daughter nodding in the pews:

yes, the light *has* changed to shadow, and yes it *has*
cast a shroud over all I once knew. Pink Floyd, how

did you know? Your stained-glass angels, their plaid
flannel wings—hell yeah, those kids were on to something.

Breaking the Broken Things

In the back room, my son is banging on his drum kit,
wailing lyrics I can't understand—something about

breaking the broken things. He's pissed off because
his kindergarten teacher told him it might snow today

in our town where snow never falls, and this morning
all he woke to was frost. So I sent him to the drums

to work it out while I type on Facebook with Janice
and Cory, playing a heavyweight bout of who can

embarrass themselves more. Today's theme: childhood
pets, the missing and the dead. I go first: 1978, after

my dog ran away, I cried every time I heard the theme song
to WKRP in Cincinnati: *Baby, if you ever wondered,*

wondered whatever became of me . . . Next up: Janice.
In third grade, her cat died, and for weeks she sang

"I Know I'll Never Love This Way Again," *mostly*
in my head, she says, *but probably also a little bit*

out loud. Cory claims he doesn't have a pet song story,
but now somehow he wishes he did, which opens up

a hole for a joke. Waiting for it, I remember the morning
my son burst into tears for reasons unknown,

how I found him sitting on the toilet, jammies bunched
around ankles, chin trembling on his bare chest,

while in the kitchen Gloria Gaynor vowed survival
to a disco beat. *It's just so sad*, he said, *how they*

loved each other and now they don't. Oh childhood,
you asshole, you unconscionable purveyor of loss.

On my computer, Janice suggests, *Cory, you could*
buy a hamster then accidentally lose it while singing

"All by Myself," and I imagine the three of us busting out
laughing like we used to years ago, leaning against

the back wall at Hemlock Tavern, a guitar solo
from someone's roommate's friend's band, perforating

our ear drums. But now Janice is in Poland, Cory in Berlin,
and I am still here with this kid who has splintered the tip

off his drumstick, pounding out a song about broken things,
in a city where promised snow always refuses to fall.

III. THE HEART HAS FOUR CHAMBERS

The Heart Has Four Chambers

The meditation leader asks us to visualize
what's in our hearts right now, and I question

when that muscled fist in my chest
became a place, four chambers like rooms

in the Morgan Library—lapis columns
and horsehair plaster walls dulling

midtown Manhattan's cacophony.
Or the Catacombs of Paris, subterranean

hallways lined with precision-stacked
femurs, hollow skulls of the innocent

dead. Which brings me to the tunnel
my wife's brothers dug in a rented backyard,

big enough for five kids to crawl into
and eat butter sandwiches while their parents

filled the kitchen with cigarette smoke
and broken glass. *We're lucky the roof*

didn't collapse, she laughs. *Maybe*
it did, I think, trapping that rag doll girl

in her hand-me-down gingham frayed
at the hem. Meaning, part of us always

stays back, while the rest marches on.
Or maybe I'm the kid with mud-packed

lungs, sleeping under the concrete patio
the next tenants laid. Maybe that's why

we recognized each other at first glance
that summer the reservoir held no water,

and those two girls jumped off
the dock's dark edge, and the night sky

proffered a handful of tinfoil stars.

A Thousand Words for Goodbye

My love has blue stars needled
    up her arm, in the shape of no
        constellation. Above that

an eight-paned window of dark
    that might open for the right tools,
        maybe. From the street vendor

we bought even the rotting
    boysenberries. Walking home,
        night fog, streetcars vibrating

concrete. And then my thumb
    crushing that bruise of fruit
        between her breasts, and then

the sweet-on-the-verge-
    of-spoiling. And then my tongue
        traveling southward, and the salt

and then the tart and then those
    hinges—did I hear them winging
        open in the kitchen's hot dark?

—

Turns out that rare Chilean wine
    cost four bucks. Ciabatta and currant jam
        served on a plaid blanket, on a cliff

named Land's End. Fog horns
    warned about the burnt orange bridge.
        It was a matter of time. Frost turned

the tomato plants into brown-haired
     witches. Through the peephole: her
        sucker-punch face and a sunflower

plucked from a bucket at the corner store.

—

Your tea tree shampoo
     and a nest of hair tangled
        in the shower drain.

Two rusted v's stained
     on the porcelain sink,
        bobby pin ghosts from

our first Halloween. The big
     bang of red sauce dried
        on the kitchen wall.

The chipped edges
     of that mirror you kept
        promising to replace.

—

I invite her absence to tea.
We watch birch leaves burn

gold in November twilight.
They're really more like spears

than hearts, she says. *I still
love you*, I confess, *but*

*it's like a moth wing hiding
in cedar-scented wool.*

—

The second-hand jewelry box
        pings out the *Love Story* theme
                while the ballerina spins drunk

on her bent spring, until the brass
        key slows its counter-clockwise
                revolution, and the girl who

forgives the ripped crinoline skirt,
        the crooked pink lips, stops her own
                dance and turns the crank for more.

—

The person I made you out to be
and the woman you thought I was

slow dance like holograms projected
on the gym floor, while you and I

sit on the bleachers, arguing
about the strangers we've become.

Tell me all the pop songs aren't
peddling codependency, you say.

Tell me love is not impermanence
dressed up in fishnets and a kicky

new skirt, I reply. Silence
stretches out her arms and yawns.

Your dance-floor ghost lays her head
on my transparent shoulder. I press

my used-to-be lips to your wish-it-were mouth.

●

Each spring the hummingbird returned
to build her nest in the elm outside our window.

They're a symbol of joy, you claimed.
Nasturtiums flamed in half barrels,

kingfishers spiked the air with song,
and god help me, I almost believed you.

●

For weeks I watched your fingers
        fold the origami squares—
                knife-blade creases, cranes

with arrows for wings. Some days
      a teacup steaming on the table
            beside you, some late nights

whiskey sweating
      in a highball glass. Always
            you slid a needle through

the bird's paper heart, beading
      one after another on scarlet
            thread. A thousand times.

The whole flock dangling
      from our ceiling when I dreamed
            you painting one word on each:

yes, *no*, *sorry*, *please*, then
      the front door slamming shut,
            then those birds bursting into flight.

Love Song for the Drag Queen at Little Orphan Andy's

Your painted-on eyebrows arched like a bridge
toward starlight, your make-up an artistry I'd never

dare hope to match, especially in that two a.m. diner,
raccoon-eyed by a break-up, stubbing my cigarette

between the Saint Pauli Girl's breasts in the ashtray
on the scarred Formica countertop. Two steps away

from a cliff-dive into despair when you
sauntered over to take my order and said, *Girl,*

your hair—I'd have to pay four hundred dollars
for a wig like that. Your eyelashes butterflied

when I looked up—*What can I get for you, hon?*
—and something shimmered on my horizon,

like a streetcar approaching ahead of schedule,
headlights tunneling toward me through fog.

Fever Dream

I have always equated you
with breath, she said, then I

woke in the echo: *and longing.*
Then Dylan on the neighbor's

stereo all day, the old stuff:
pillbox hat, Maggie's farm.

Nostalgia curled on the couch
and stayed, singing harmony

with the plumes of fog swirling
across the weed-choked

garden, the raised beds
where we planted and planted,

but those cosmos never took.

Last Call

In the tin-can-string-tin-can
contraption, you speak

fluent Mandarin; I hear
a dead language

chiseled into stone
tablets dissolving

beneath the Red Sea.
Before the ER doc

unhooks her surgical mask
to pronounce us "we did

everything we know
how to do," I take up this

rummage sale sax, blow
quarter notes marked

by redwing blackbirds
arranged on phone wires

lining our street. If you
can hear me, blink

once for yes, twice for no.

Coming Home

A flash of iridescent, humming green
lingers at the hook

in the porch's crossbeam,
where the teardrop of amber glass

used to hang. Remember? The one
we bought our first June

and kept full of red nectar for years.

Prayer for Beginning

Make me the surface of an alpine lake at six a.m.,
an osprey's fish-hook body hovering above,

readying the dive. Or the moth that lands on
evening's screen door, the one that turns to dust

when you touch it. Let me be the lipstick
left in her summer-hot car, sweating on the brink

of losing my form. Or the humming bird
that buzzed at her spark-yellow t-shirt as she

knelt in the garden, clearing the soil of stones.
Oh let me, let me love her, love her here

on the precipice of Coltrane's longest note—
say it over and over again, right before it breaks.

To the First Person Who Ate an Artichoke

Snipping the gold barbs
    off the outer leaves,

rubbing their tough skin
    soft with oil, garlic

pulp, then salt, I wonder
    what hunger drove you

down past the thistle's
    dry chokes, that spiked,

protective fur, believing
    all the while in this

meaty green heart.

The Gospel According to Sky

No matter how many times I hear them,
I cannot remember the names of clouds—

not the brush strokes whipping upward
like a wishing breath, not the cotton batting

sculpted by morning's light, nor the low-hung
burnished steel that insulates, compresses

like mood. The encyclopedia sings cirrus,
stratus, cumulus, cirrocumulus, altostratus,

altocumulus, cumulonimbus, stratocumulus,
but all I recall is how the immutable blue

holds those changing shapes, like a lover
who's finally learned how to love her right.

IV. THAT I COULD KEEP YOU LIKE THIS

Still Life, Ocean Beach

Ring-billed gulls pick at the dead
    seal's flesh, its ivory skeleton
        emerging like sculpture

from stone: jaw line, ribcage,
    the intricate fin bones looking
        too much like human feet.

Fog holds the death stench close.
    Up ahead, a silhouette of a woman
        toeing yellow foam left behind

by the retracting tide. She could be
    fishing, except she holds nothing
        but a tremor in her hands, finger

pressed to her lips like she's
    forgotten something and can't
        decide if she wants to go back.

Paint-spattered work jacket,
    salt-crusted knuckles, black hair
        hanging like kelp fronds slick

with grief. Neck craned
    downward, she studies the sand,
        as if those ground up bits of shell

could spell out an answer,
    or even the right question,
        in a language she might know.

In the Ocean Some Survive by Drowning

She wore a dripping wig of bees
      as she needled copper

filament through fingernails
      the nightmare had removed

while she feigned sleep.

> *Madness writes too many*
> *songs for the sirens*
> *to quit their jawing.*

In the barbed net of her
      dream, she snagged

her own open mouth
      submerged and sinking.

The locked box insists

on its emptiness. That it is
imaginary and resting

on the plumped-up lining
of your uterus means

nothing. In the night, longing
folded up her circus tent

and skipped town, leaving
behind a list of organs

the body can live without:
gall bladder, appendix, spleen.

How many times?
You, lying there alone,

wanting the wanting
to return, brass skeleton key

tethered to her waist.

Some Days Are Skin as Tinfoil

Some days are lips nursing
     the wire monkey's tit.

Some dusks are a disk-flat
     moon charged electrical

above the shark tooth
     mountain crest. Some

hollows are the sound
     of a fist pounding

on the door of the vacant
     house that is called

your body, with its
     shuttered windows,

grove of redwoods
     waving manic

in the silver-black
     wind. Some bodies

are nights holding stars
     as puncture wounds.

Some nights are no route in.

What You Were Doing Up There

That house, that roof—
        above your mother's
                porcelain angels who

saved no souls, shingles
        threatening splinters
                to your tender feet.

Recording the decibel level
        of the space between
                voice and echo is what

you said you were doing
        up there. Funeral incense
                cleaves the lungs, stars

whispering behind veils
        of cloud. *Detecting red light*
                from a gas-poor galaxy

is what you said you were
        doing up there—words
                tweezed from misfiring

synapses. *Atmospheric*
        ram pressure lighting
                the fuse is how a meteor

burns. Your mind crafting
        its mosaic out of shattered
                mirrors, your compass needle

stuttering toward some other home.

That I Could Keep You Like This

That you were
    falling, we all knew.

        How sound travels across
            a morning lake is how

        I hear voices calling
            always—that's what you

        need to remember about me.

That you have fallen
is a fact the water

will neither swallow
nor erase.

        Trust this: You will
            not understand me

        when I stitch sound
            in the language of my mind.

The last time you left,
    I carried your glass

to the sink, dunked it
    in soapy water. That your

fingerprints sifted upward
    like lace is what I imagined,

that I could pinch them up
    off the water's surface,

press them to my lips—

    A distance, by definition,
      cannot be closed,

    not even by sound.

—is what I dreamed.

A Million Silver Minnows

Unzipping the baggy velvet dress
     revealed three layers of t-shirts

padding your scalloped
     vertebrae, your secret ribs.

Can you recommend
     a book that will make me

like being a woman?

A cocktail party marionette,
     drug hooks edging up

the corners of your lips,
     you were trying to fashion

a person out of glass.
     You were trying to construct

Tokyo in a lost bottle. You were
     trying your best to survive,

always in clothes that didn't fit.

Could you say it?
     Could you say

the knees bloodied
     on graveled streets,

the elaborate tortures
         of reluctant saints,

his hands slick as Iowa
         river rock, the summer

of dropped knives—
         could you say it

all added up? I have
         tried. Arithmetic

does not ease pain.

How you spoke: gesturing
         with open hands, slow motion

wave of the faithfully departing.

         Because you can know
                  only what you

         would do in my
                  situation, you will

         never comprehend
                  why I have done

         what I have done.

And so it's over—
      the mandolin's umber

curves, the fissured
      varnish, the notes

that longed to enter,
      always nibbling

at your skin, a million
      silver minnows,

a school of impotent songs.

Halfway Up Devil Mountain

Among the horsefly buzz
　　and lizard tails whipping
　　　　fallen leaves, not a single

human sound in this forest,
　　save your own labored
　　　　breath. Remember when

words came as easily
　　as mosquitoes to still
　　　　water? Neither do I.

Blackberry vines, weighted
　　by summer's final fruit,
　　　　depend into a trickling stream.

Spiders crochet hammocks
　　between the dry weeds.
　　　　Light plays on them

like an invitation. Admit it:
　　last night a dream child
　　　　sang to you about a rabbit

howling its wolf-heart
　　at the moon. Last night's
　　　　dream whispered, *It's time.*

Fold your own paper boat and set sail.

V. THE ACROBATS OF PITTSBURGH

The Acrobats of Pittsburgh

A medevac helicopter descends diagonally
across my hotel window, all blue metal

and yellow warning lights, scaring off
the hospital roof an explosion of pigeons

who scatter like shrapnel then regroup
in the air as one body flying.

—

Last week my father fell down a flight
of stairs—hear the compression of ribcage

against risers, the forced exhalation
of breath, skull hitting stone, knocking

a blood stain onto a CT scan, landing him
on an airlift to Stanford's neurology wing.

—

Last night I boarded an airplane that flew me
three thousand miles away from my kids.

First time. Eastbound jets accelerate nightfall,
snowcaps blushing amber then dark, and no,

that death symbol wasn't lost on me.

—

Those pigeons kamikaze diving in the cold
blue over Pittsburgh are the same color

as their shadows gliding across the city's
brick and glass façade, except for the talc

white one in the center who seems to be
the axis on which all the others turn.

—

Your father is fine now, my mother said
when she called to tell me the news, *but*

he had a little accident last week. Though
I live an hour from that hospital, though

I could have been there to hold his hand
or hers, she called a week too late, which

begs the question, *What else don't I know?*

—

The helicopter has disappeared behind
a skyscraper, touched down on the pad

and cut power. The pigeons return to
their ledge, perch like gargoyles and wait.

—

My kids still believe that dying happens
to old people, even after the eldest read

Abraham Lincoln's birth and death dates
then did the math. He concluded, *This*

president must not have taken very good
care of himself. I blinked twice. I said nothing.

—

A glassed-in footbridge stretches over the road
below my hotel window. Across it an orderly

guides an empty gurney. A stooped patient
pushes her IV pole. A man in a wheelchair

rolls halfway across then pauses, looks down
at traffic clogging the street.

—

On the speaker phone, I tell the kids
The pigeons here sail through the sky

like acrobats. The youngest says, *I can do that,*
and takes off to perform tricks I can't see.

The older one says, *There are two thousand*
words in my Spanish dictionary, and I like

the index best. Those words burst forward in flocks.
I ask him to look up *airplane, telephone, bird.*

—

Why does anyone ever leave anyone they love?

—

Imagine picking your way down
an unlit hallway, feeling the walls

for a switch: bare foot stepping
on hardwood plank then

bare foot stepping on air.
Dad and I haven't talked about

the accident, except when I said,
I am buying you a headlamp

and a GPS for your next trip
through the dark. And he laughed.

And then we were silent.

—

My son texts the words: *avion, telephono, pajaro.*

—

Sometimes you have to let people fall.

—

A bird trainer once told me no one knows for sure
how homing pigeons find their way back—

maybe something about metal granules in their ears
interacting with earth's magnetic force.

—

On the street, an ambulance siren fires off
like a starting gun, and those birds, they're at it

again, trapeze artists launching off platforms,
swinging arcs only nature could design.

Notes to Myself on the Morning after His Birth

That particular color of his skin,
      revealed like a sunset through

sooted glass as you rubbed
      the vernix in—you will never

see it again. Or his body's
      plumpness in the first hours,

like a cake's perfect rise held only
      for a moment, as if on the breath

of god before the exhale—you will
      never get that back. Nor will it ever

leave you. And though you could
      never recreate the sound you made

last night, gripped in labor's throes—
      something between tiger growl

and lamb bleat—the noise that
      hooked your consciousness,

dragged you away from the birth beast
      just long enough to think *Is that*

me? Long enough to know *I am*
      fighting death for you—though you

won't ever hear it again, you will
      never forget how this morning

the infant nestled in your arms
        echoed the exact timbre

and rhythm of that sound,
        marking you his, naming you

home. Mama, be warned,
        you have signed on to witness

a daily parade of exquisite
        losses. They will move through

your body like the Doppler swell
        of orgasm, or the flavor of August-

ripe blackberries that will, if you
        hold them long enough, write

the story of their soil on your tongue.

Diagnosis

Those crimson patches of scaly skin
      flaring under your blue eyes—
            you think one looks like Guam

and the other Oahu on the maps
      you love. The doctor's note reads
            Lupus, question mark tacked

on the end like a donkey's tail, and I
      wonder, *With all the genetic options*
            spread out in that storefront

window, how could we
      have picked this? The Pacific
            shrugs that inquiry off her foamy

shoulders, pulls back as the moon
      commands. And you, five years old
            with a needle stuck in your vein,

the phlebotomist's gloved hand
      anaconda-wrapped around your wrist—
            you burrow your wet face into my neck

and scream, *I don't want this,*
      I don't want this, I don't want this,
            while I watch your blood spray

into the collection tube and whisper,
      Say it again, say it again, as if
            your voice could rewrite the code.

Don't

Don't think about white blood cells
chewing up his lung tissue, like termites

gorging on dry rot. Don't think about
your grandmother's oxygen tank

or the pediatric gas mask her genes—
your genes—have fit over his small face.

Don't think about how he believes
his peak flow monitor is a cool toy

the pulmonologist gave him. Don't
think about the Statue of Liberty

he sculpted out of yellow modeling clay
then annotated with ballpoint ink: *head,*

baby growing in belly, vagina, torch.
Don't let it remind you of the innkeepers

in Ireland who had hung their dead child's
watercolors on their guestroom walls.

Think instead about the hours he spent
on the beach last weekend, digging

a giant pit in the sand, then pratfalling
into it, over and over, in slow motion.

No. Don't think about that either.
Not the hole. Not the falling.

Vocabulary

Las Trampas Creek has swallowed
      a two-slice chrome toaster and a yellow bike
            with a wire basket, like newspaper delivery boys

used to ride. Climbing the bridge railing,
      my kid says, *Small airplanes have straight wings*
            pointing left and right, or east and west. I say,

Yes, that's called 'perpendicular to the fuselage.'
      Always I want to offer him something lasting
            and good, but today all I've got is vocabulary.

So he rolls those pebbles of sound around
      in his mouth, while we watch two Canada geese
            move like captain-less clipper ships, writing

S-patterns in green water, until a bus rushes by,
      sending eddies of oak leaves spiraling down
            the sidewalk, and we follow them, walking

home under wind-stripped branches,
      distant call of that migrating flock bugling
            toward us, ripping open winter's gray sky.

Get Ready

Who's to say the hammered brass fish
    welded to those wrought iron waves
        won't break free—the whole school

turning flesh, swimming elliptical
    ribbons in the ocean overhead?
        The sea anemone in your chest

opens—tentacles undulating
    in tide pool sluices—then clenches
        shut on its prey, or the finger poke

of fear. Who's to say an egret won't let up
    out of the marshland weeds, gracious
        white shock to the sky, and set your own

wings beating toward some light?

The Problem Is

You believe you are bone
       and blood, the weighted
              organs, wax-yellow

pounds of fat. The concerns
       of your family looped
              around your neck

like a yoke of giant kelp
       dragging you seaward.
              What if you're not

the seventy-eight percent
       water you've read about,
              but a canoe-shaped

feather riding its waves?
       Not matter forced to earth
              by gravity, but the air

through which it falls?

How to Swim Naked in a Night Lake

Remember this is all you have wanted:
the ladder's algae-slick rungs

soothing your summer-cracked feet,
the lake's onyx mouth

swallowing you whole—bruised
legs, round hips, exhausted breasts.

Midnight's moonless dome will pulse
darkness pinned with light, as you

stroke to the center, roll belly-up
and float. Breathe, your lungs' cadence

rising and falling. Thatched raft,
lost doll, whim to the ripple's wake—

stay, your flotsam heart pounding
above the catfish spikes, the hidden teeth.

How to Slice Bananas

Never mind how
the open-mouthed oven

begs for bread
or how the blender

will liquefy this flesh
for the children's

always-hunger.
The house is quiet now.

Just this moment's
infinite expanse

and your thumb
pressing the sweet

yellow weight
against the blade.

His Currency

He slathers rocks with gold acrylic
squeezed from a wrinkled tube,

stacks them on my altar, like pebbles
the living place on headstones

to communicate about the dead:
She was visited; I was here.

He was here: curled on my now
bony chest, howling wet being

I pulled from my open wound.
My animal nose, pressed to his

vernix-waxed scalp, breathed in
the best answer to every question

I know. *Love*—I ask him to write
the word, in his shaky script,

and I tape it above my desk,
so when the bills stack up

and the unknown lurks
like a trap door switch waiting

to be tripped, I can read it
again and remember again

all I have forgotten.

Melodrama of the Suburban Kindergartener

You would think I had asked him to swim
        naked across an alligator-spiked swamp,

my son whom I have sent walking across
        a flat acre of asphalt, to his classroom,

alone. Though I pressed language
        into his hand: *this feels scary, but it's not*

dangerous; you are taking one
        for the team, twenty-five yards in,

he looks back at me and melts his face
        into a tragedy mask. This morning

his aunt is losing her breasts to cancer.
        He doesn't know. This morning Cairo

has erupted into chaos. He has
no idea. How many kids ate hunger

for breakfast? In the car, his sick brother
        coughs spit into a cup, while I watch

my blond boy shuffle away from me,
        molasses pace and sobbing. This is where

survival begins: that boy finally crossing
        his threshold, this mom letting him go.

Instinct

Scientists theorize
she had suffered

the devastating
loss of a cub,

the lioness nudging
the antelope calf

toward water,
that one hunger

devouring all others.

The Words Are

A black-shelled sea snail
  steamed in salt water. Stab

the sealed hole with a pin,
  pries the cooked worm out.

Repeat. The words are:
  brain tumor, cancerous,

inoperable. Repeat: the pin's
  insertion, the elaborate

untangling from opalescent
  coils, the kitchen table

littered with empty shells.
  Repeat. Again. Again,

in this land between
  dream and waking, where

thought can make it real:
  the pin tip pricking

the dark object, a skilled
  hand snaking it out.

—

Headline: *Tsunami Aftershocks Reach*
California's Harbors. Rain floods

Watsonville's strawberry fields.
The water the storm leaves behind

becomes ragged mirrors of sky, earth
holding space hostage. Today

is my friend's thirty-third birthday.
In lieu of gifts: *neurological oncology*,

palliative chemotherapy. All day,
waves cross the television screens,

blanketing Japan in roils of foam, erasing
the bicycles, the road signs and cars.

Again: the lungs flushed with salt water.
Repeat: the wrists gripped then let go.

—

A shopkeeper slugs through her drowned
inventory. Eggplant undergoes radiation

testing. The Pacific collects rafts of debris.
The death toll upticks to nineteen thousand,

while a single silver pine, bowing over
Japan's landscape, dreams of fallen trees.

—

The words are: *glioma,*
midbrain, incurable.

Change the right word,
and they can save her.

No. I'm not kidding. Get out
your red pen, whoever

you are, and change one.

—

The words are: *Spring*
    arrived today, with all her
        spangled light. My friend's

treatments have not
    begun yet. She still looks
        healthy. Aside from the cancer,

she's healthy. The words
    are: *Tragedy can't happen*
        under such blue skies.

Grand oaks regenerating
    their leaves, tulips raising red
        cups to the sun. The words are:

Yes it can.

—

Nine days after the tsunami,
a dolphin is rescued

from a rice paddy
fifteen miles from shore.

The words are: *if, then*.

——

The leopard print chiffon scarf
blown into a puddle on the road,

the half-dead Painted Lady
waving one orange and black wing

on her driveway: do not read these
as symbols. Carry the take-out bag

to her doorstep. Ring the bell.
Watch the goldfinch alight

on a cherry branch, petals
raining down on the walkway.

The words are: *No one knows*
what will happen. The words are:

Love your people like this
stark light bathing the land.

Lake Dharma

You arrive at the lake, expecting
to meet grief on the trail.

Instead: a fleet of white pelicans
patrolling the shallows, steam

rising off the water glow.
Cormorants on the watchtower

moan and tick, indifferent
wings shrugged toward the sun.

Not even the day moon, having
dusted off last week's rusty eclipse,

cares to hear your story
of a marriage slowly crumbling,

a young friend lost to cancer.
Then another. And another.

This whole forest depends
on that felled tree rotting into

home for salamander eggs,
centipedes, six varieties of moss.

Black phoebes rattle winter
thistles, swollen throats percussing:

this is, this is, this is . . .

Notes

Epigraphs: Lao Tzu's quotation is sourced from Stephen Mitchell's translation of *Tao Te Ching*, chapter 15; Grace Paley's quotation is sourced from an interview with the *Paris Review*, "The Art of Fiction No. 131."

"Good Morning Heartache" borrows its title from Billy Holiday's classic tune, written by Irene Higginbotham, Ervin Drake, and Dan Fisher.

"The Red-Shouldered Hawk, the Raven" is for Deema Shehabi.

"Breaking the Broken Things" is for Cory and Janice. It includes a line from the theme song from *WKRP in Cincinnati*. Composed by Tom Wells, with lyrics by Hugh Wilson, and performed by Steve Carlisle, the song was released as a 45 rpm vinyl single, by MCA Records, in 1979.

"Vocabulary" is for Brennan.

"His Currency" is for Kian.

"The Words Are" is for Susan.

Acknowledgments

Thanks to the editors of the following journals, in which many of these poems were published, sometimes in earlier versions:

Ampersand Review ("The Flock," "Halfway Up Devil Mountain," "Last Call," "The locked box insists," "Showtime at the Ministry of Lost Causes," "Some Days Are Skin as Tinfoil"); *Bayou Magazine* ("When she finally lost the weight"); *Bloom* ("Conception Myth," "The Heart Has Four Chambers"); *Connotation Press* ("On Air Guitar, Lip Gloss and Flat Irons," "A Thousand Words for Goodbye"); *Fourth River* ("How to Swim Naked in a Night Lake"); *Literary Mama* ("Breaking the Broken Things," "Don't," "His Currency"); *Pea River Journal* ("Colossal Failure of Human Design, We Celebrate the 100th Anniversary of Your Death," "It's not the Holy Spirit," "Love Song for the Drag Queen at Little Orphan Andy's," "Still Life, Ocean Beach," "When There's No Money Left"); *Poetry East* ("The Red-Shouldered Hawk, the Raven"); *Raleigh Review* ("Revolution"); *Redheaded Stepchild* ("The Gospel According to Clouds"); *Santa Clara Review* ("Lake Dharma"); *Sou'wester* ("The Problem Is").

"Ode to October" appears in the anthology *Follow the Thread*, edited by Alan Cohen, benefitting the Power of Poetry and Wellspring of Imagination programs, in Logan, Ohio.

"A Thousand Words for Goodbye" appears in the anthology *Shared Light*, edited by Christine Richardson, benefitting The Willow Glen Poetry Project, in San Jose, California.

Sometimes it takes only a few well-timed words of encouragement to keep a writer going. Much gratitude to these writers who, whether they know it or not, said the right thing at exactly the right time: Kim Addonizio, Jan Beatty, Sean Thomas Dougherty,

Lynn Emanuel, Steve Fellner, John Hoppenthaler, Dorianne Laux, Michael Martone, and Aaron Smith.

Thank you also to the writers Judy French, Laura Headley, Susan Goldberg, and Deema Shehabi for your sustaining friendship, literary conversation, and wicked good senses of humor.

Thank you to superfriends Becky Cable, Elisa Dumesnil, Susan Nachand, Gabby Seagrave, LaDonna Silva, and Heidi Wiltsee for your ever-reliable love, laughter, smarts, and support.

Thank you to my village, who have watched over my kids (and me) and helped make my writing time possible, including the Barbier family, all the Dumesnils, the French-Byrne family, the Havrelinko family, the Lagaya family, Angela Silva, the Wharton family, and all aforementioned superfriends.

To Tracie Vickers, thank you for your unwavering support as I built this book.

Brennan and Kian, thank you for your ongoing patience while I am writing. Seriously, dudes. Thank you for inspiring me and making me laugh, loudly, every day. For real. I love you, my monsters.

To Sarah Richmond, "*lost* and *soul* and *mate* and *found*," my eternal gratitude for your love, support, courage, and grace.